A Drill Sergeant's Fame

A Drill Sergeant's Fame

When soldier recruits graduate basic combat training, everything they become is attributed to the effective training of their drill sergeants. *A Drill Sergeant's Fame* displays this concept and more.

Kimberly Mae

authorHOUSE®

AuthorHouse™
1663 Liberty Drive
Bloomington, IN 47403
www.authorhouse.com
Phone: 1-800-839-8640

© 2015 Kimberly Mae. All rights reserved.

No part of this book may be reproduced, stored in a retrieval system, or transmitted by any means without the written permission of the author.

Published by AuthorHouse   09/25/2015

ISBN: 978-1-4918-7032-7 (sc)
ISBN: 978-1-4918-7033-4 (hc)
ISBN: 978-1-4918-7034-1 (e)

Library of Congress Control Number: 2014904364

Print information available on the last page.

Any people depicted in stock imagery provided by Thinkstock are models, and such images are being used for illustrative purposes only.
Certain stock imagery © Thinkstock.

This book is printed on acid-free paper.

Because of the dynamic nature of the Internet, any web addresses or links contained in this book may have changed since publication and may no longer be valid. The views expressed in this work are solely those of the author and do not necessarily reflect the views of the publisher, and the publisher hereby disclaims any responsibility for them.

Contents

The Hero

A Hero's Sacrifice	3
A Drill Sergeant's Fame	6
Troops Seen through Another's Eye	9
To the End	12
The Soldier's Guardian	14
Irony within a Combat Bunker	18
Innocence Reborn	21

Overseas with 101

Forever Untwined	25
The Fatuous Kind	27
Afghanistan Beauty or Boils	30
Treachery from Within	33
Life's Fear or Fate's Glory Tear	36
Cavernous Vile Remnants	39
Anticipation Changing	41
Inner Peace Now Unleashed	44

Basic Combat Training

Our Own Fight	49
Madness	52
Fashioned Just Right	55
Hasty Decisions	57
Man Up	60

Army Owned	63
Born and Bred American Soldier	65
Freedom Killers	68

The Transcendent

Epiphany's Edge	77
A Joyful Tale	79
A Memory's Whisper	82
A Heart's Mend	84
Memories End	87
Love's Cruel Passion	89
Inept Dreams	92

A Special Thanks

Incessant Love	95
Bittersweet	98

Dedications

To the Philanthropic Everlasting
Deity & Especially
To all our Fallen Soldiers

Your precious memories are forever embedded
into the hearts and souls of everyone who knew
you. Thank you for your service and dedication
to our country. You are not forgotten.

To all the Drill Sergeants and servicemen
and women around the world, thank
you for your diligence and sacrifice. You
make this world a better place.

To my parents Frances and Robert and to my family, especially Glenn, Michael, Caleb and Riddick- Thank you for your love and support.

"Impossible is nothing."
T. J.

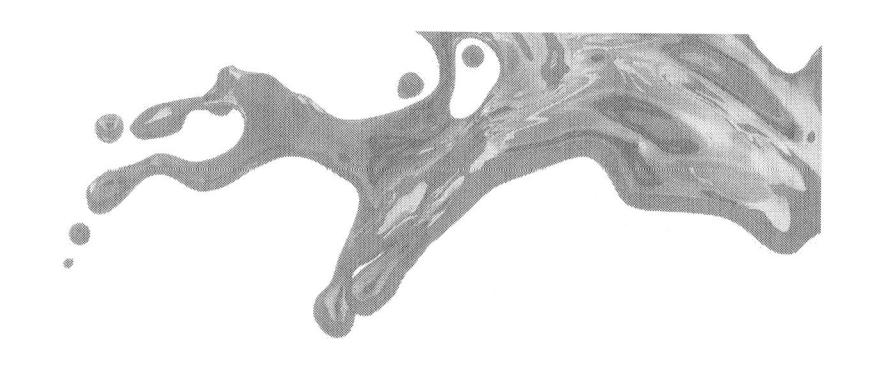

The Hero

A Hero's Sacrifice

An honor to fight, marching into war—
Sights fixed rock hard, down to the core.
Nothing exotic, though our army is the best.
Uniformed and critiqued, for some, here comes final rest.
American soldiers in combat, please don't shed one tear;
We're suited up, professional warriors without fear.
Climbing mountains, dodging bullets, emotions not mixed—
Face-to-face, piercing daggers earnestly fixed.
Here wrongs are made right, hard as it may seem;
Soldiers bravely face this for their team.
Proving themselves honorable souls who pay the ultimate price.
Their own lives, through their eyes, are a small sacrifice.
Looking upon others pillaged and scorned,
Their hearts grow black, yearning to mourn.
Those not knowing peace or joy once foretold,
Are living in a callous globe dark and cold.
Soldiers with courage, faith, and a passionate drive—
Our malice-filled enemies make sure they don't stay alive.
All the while warriors' hearts held high, purposely to defend
Our God-given freedom, right down to their bloody end.
The heroes' sacrifice is now revealed:
Giving their lives out in the field.
Their sole purpose is duty, honor, integrity, and respect—
Thus, the greatest men on earth have such profound effects.
Many will strive but none could ever compare
To fallen soldiers—don't even dare!

Months went by during our deployment to Afghanistan before a soldier in our unit died in combat. As is custom, we stood shoulder to shoulder in two separate parallel ranks or lines, saluting while the body of our fallen soldier was passed between us on a litter (a basic form of a stretcher) covered by the American flag. When our hero passed by me, I began to silently let loose tears. As soon as we dropped our salutes and departed from the HLZ (helicopter landing zone), I ran to my room to further pay respect by writing this poem, "A Hero's Sacrifice."

Notes

A Drill Sergeant's Fame

The drill sergeants we've come to know
Are prodigies at making us feel low.
For their voices do precisely yell
To viciously dish out hell.
They love to exclaim, "Beat your face!"
We'd like to put in their eyes just a bit of Mace.
'Tis a vengeful thought for now;
I'm sure they have a secret calculating vow.
And while running the two-mile race,
Our drill sergeants will be all up in our face.
"Hey, you re-re, you're such a window licker!
You better move those legs quicker!"
That's our drill sergeants' way;
They make us ball our fists and say,
"You rode the short bus, not I.
We can tell by the demon in your eye."
Our drill sergeants then cynically confess,
"Down in the dirt, you hot mess!"
All to trigger hot-blooded progress.
It makes us heated, but we do our best.
Our push-ups and sit-ups prove just the same.
All the while our drill sergeants scream,
"Yeah, can't believe you came!
Go down farther, get up, and do more!
If you can't, we'll throw your ass out the door!"

Now pause to realize their dark, piercing eyes
Just might tell a tale of lies,
For a sweeter side is known by their kin.
To us, the soldier recruits, it's hidden deep within-
Purposely done for their battle buddies to shield,
Making us soldiers to survive in the field.

So now at their best, they'll be seen downrange,
Together in combat, killing without shame.
Stop and realize we'll be filled with pride
To be fighting so fiercely, right at their side.
Then and there this won't lie:
Thank you, Drill Sergeants,
For this long and ludicrous ride!

    Near the end of basic training, one of my battle buddies told everyone, including our drill sergeants, about my writing poetry, naming this poem in particular. There I was, standing in front of forty or so soldiers in training and about three drill sergeants. Stuttering, with sweat pouring down my face, I read it aloud at their command, dreading the consequence. To my amazement, I received good reviews but then was told to "beat my face" (get down to do push-ups) for swearing (in the original version).

A Drill Sergeant's Fame

Notes

Troops Seen through Another's Eye

First sergeant (1SG) tactically overseeing the rest,
Through his eyes seen not as the best.
His main concern, one zero zero or two zero five,*
Tracking his soldiers, keeping them alive.
Physically and mentally this holds true,
Monitoring pay, promotions, and family too.
Applying when needed the proper factor,
In efforts to progress his soldiers' moral protractor.
Meant to discern with never-ending grace,
Gauging many a different face,
To notice those whose maturity and judgment lack,
Trying to decrease a negative impact.
Informative chats and corrective training,
Supposed to entail positives, minus shaming.
But the soldiers proven at first sight
Physically fit to withstand 1SG's fight,
Adding a showcase of motivation and drive,
Mitigating notions of leadership and jive.

Soldiers beneath are far more valuable,
Their works never to be seen as scrabble.
1SG toils to find each soldier's place
Within this respected yet torturous race.
Earnestly fixing any and all faults,
Time then reveals satisfying results.

Proven true when calls come in from men-
First Sergeant, five years past you lent a hand;
May I now ask for your services, once again?

* The third line, "one zero zero (100) or two zero five (205,)" references typically the number of soldiers in one company a 1SG is responsible for. This was, in particular, the smallest to largest number of soldiers my 1SG came across to command during his career.

One day while deployed to Afghanistan, I noticed my1SG was gazing out into the mountains. As I walked past, I turned and asked him if he needed anything. He looked at me and said, "You write poetry, Nero, right? Why not write one about a 1SG?"

I thought that would be intriguing, so we met in his office later the next day during lunch. I asked questions while conducting an interview and formed his answers into this poem.

I still wonder what was on his mind that day 1SG was captivated by the scenery of Afghanistan, gazing off into the distant land. I guess I'll never know.

Notes

To the End

Choppers heard flying overhead;
Once again a soldier wound up dead.
Giving his life, one of the better few,
Those alive and well do salute.
Twenty-one bullets heard by all,
Honoring the soldiers who fall.
Hearts that once beat to a survivor's tune,
Now seen through the shadow of a moon.
Tears that fall are mixed with sorrow and pride;
Emotions run past like a powerful riptide,
With eyes wide open, seeing souls that defend,
Who give their lives honorably to the end.

   I wrote this poem in the hall of our living quarters. I sat on the ground, upset and pretty much in a foul mood altogether. I had heard of a soldier who died in combat, and a flood of rage engrossed me. An enormous assortment of profane words filled my head. I angrily put pen to paper, wanting to express a heated and obscene thought, but instead a poem crashed out of me. Later, back in the States, I gave it this title, "To the End."

Notes

The Soldier's Guardian

A family of three known as one
Lives in the clouds to ensure a job well done.
Keeping watch, our savior and maker,
Though disbelieved, the son restrains the unearthly taker.
Out in the field, detoured but not lost,
A life not meant to pay the ultimate cost.
It seems this day encompassed by loss,
Minds trodden down with many a thought.
Then by a miracle this instant proves anew.
Something wondrous and glorious too:
The soldier left not by plan
Now doing a job that seems as no man can.
All alone, some may say.
But come to know that very same day,
A man not on earth held higher than the rest
All the while was in his midst a guest.
Camouflaged into a shade of black,
Amazingly done with such great tact.
Shielded for no eye to see,
This soldier hidden beneath a tree,
Strong and brave down to his core,
Nobody but one shall know about his score.
His guardian above to mend a soul,
Also keeps danger from taking its toll.
Steadfast and safe, never to lie,
No enemy will see his face or his eye.
A yard or two from this soldier's right,

Still nowhere within the devil's sight.
This warrior hidden alive and well,
Soon to reunite, having a miraculous tale to tell.
A delightful story not always so,
For by this it's made known-
The universe is destined with each depraved blow.
Flying by, a life is taken while we're below;
Now this soldier lives- a spirit in the sky,
Watching your back, by and by,
Far atop the wind and rain,
Peering down from a different plane.
It was his time, the only answer shown.
War brings pain, as every soldier knows.
A promise of wealth in happiness and being
Is found to not always mean that one is breathing.
Torture passed no captive here;
Alive and well, his soul absent of fear.

One night while deployed, a story began to float about that we lost a soldier, literally. Soon thereafter, male soldiers were getting ready for a rescue mission, while the female soldiers were being tasked with mundane jobs within our walls of protection. After our delegated tasks were complete, I went to my room with a heavy heart. I lay on my stomach and began to write, with the eye of my spirit guiding my pen.

Originally I thought this soldier would come back alive and well. I felt it in my soul, a sort of peaceable rest. Later, when word came in that this soldier didn't make it back alive, I lost my bearings. I wanted to rewrite the poem but instead just added to the end.

I heard later that our hero was found at the base of a tree and had died fighting, killing many insurgents around him. I also was told that the enemy was planning on backtracking to take our soldier captive and torture him on television for the entire world to witness. Thankfully, this never came to pass—hence, the second to last line, "Torture passed no captive here."

In retrospect, many times in life we have a definitive answer for what is a good, acceptable, or bad outcome, yet we fail to see all the other issues and possibilities in between. Happiness and peace can creep through the darkest of situations in unexpected ways and answers, if we are open to seeing and understanding them.

Notes

Irony within a Combat Bunker

A concrete tunnel filled with soldiers and men,
Numbers that are more or less than ten.
Shoulder to shoulder though spirits are high,
Presuming that everyone will pass death by.
Incredible and astonishing this remembrance is,
All soldiers producing a soul-estranged kiss.
As bombs are heard landing and launching,
They all sit content, no one watching—
Some eating and drinking, lacking fear and thought,
Others joking without a care or thinking one fought.
Stories then are quickly shared, making the time swiftly pass.
Now some playfully let loose a left hook fast;
More mischief follows with chips and rocks tossed about.
Boom! Loud and thunderous is then felt and heard,
Yet no one bats an eye or utters a concerning word.
Lightheartedness continues on with a happy bliss;
Over the radio it's heard—all is clear, personnel may go amiss.
A soldier exclaims, "Damn it," with a cold scowl.
"This workday I've just now lost an hour."
During these moments one C.O.P.* over,
A different tone is real, praying for a four-leaf clover.
There, a soldier is bleeding and down,
Many within those walls wearing a frown.
Some may say, learn to pray, mindful of that hour.
Don't be distracted, a selfish kind of coward.
Think on this for a moment before throwing a sharp spear.
What else is there to do but exist with hope detouring fear?

So those in that second to spread a disease
Realize help comes from above and fate's knocking, so please,
Listen up, and listen good;
What else would you do if you could?
Soldiers are trained, and this we know,
To keep our heads on straight and our hearts not low.
Then a watchful eye with quick reaction time,
Your brother in arms alive, much more costly than a dime.
A steady hand and sharp eye, a soldier's soul-draining job,
No matter the situation or moral on their C.O.P. or F.O.B.*
Jokes and laughter help to carry out what's to be;
Don't judge—we're here to make this world fit for your family.

*C.O.P: combat outpost; smaller than a-
**F.O.B: forward operating base.

    This interesting memory includes me and other soldiers with civilians in a bunker (a large concrete tunnel built to shield soldiers when taking incoming artillery from the enemy) during an attack. I thought about what this situation might look like from a deviated point of view and logged it in my mind, later forming this poem.

Notes

INNOCENCE REBORN

Once my heart was torn,
Copious instances of sorrow to mourn.
Time then mysteriously amended,
Every occurrence perfectly connected.
With eyes wide open, moving forth,
Bursting with gladness, an exuding force.
My love meant to never grow coarse—
Now to be altered, set for dissimilar direct.
Destiny's face implausibly revealed,
A neoteric future with infinite zeal.
How would you say this came to be?
My story now for all to see.

Distraught, helpless, feeling alone—
Another noticing, moving into the zone.
Now in her midst, a man with drive,
Ensuing her innermost being, making alive;
A childlike trust innocence reborn.
Her countenance can now finally adorn.
Eyes beholding magnificent visions,
Once thought to be idiotic conflictions.
This journey's morphed and recreated,
A dreary mind full of sorrow—forever faded;
Determination and wonders, ambition effusively changed,
Her life's tale lavishly rearranged.

Notes

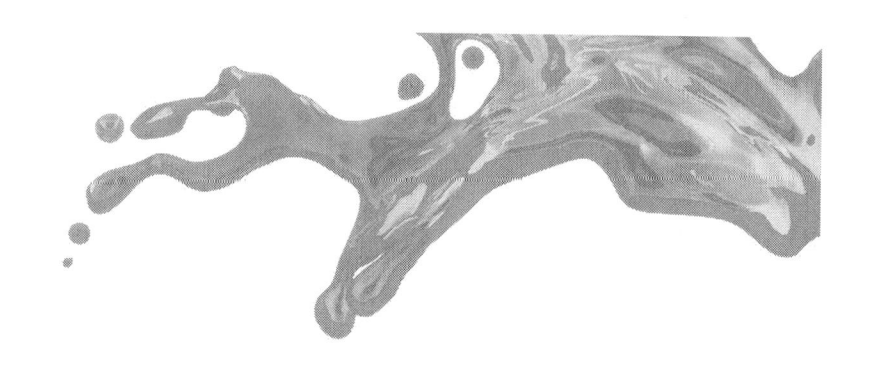

Overseas with 101

Forever Untwined

Sometimes a soul's yearning is to simply forget.

What I hold in my heart, 'tis true, man should ne'er tell;
These pictures and sounds, one ought not take out of its shell.
So deep within buried they lie, grudgingly clinging to my soul,
Rotting away a sweet fragrance that once filled this empty hole.
No more shall my spirit and body be refuge for all that seems kind,
That which was once has now become forever untwined.

This poem came to me in the middle of the night, telling of the images that seared my soul and left a lasting impression I'll never forget. I was out at a C.O.P. in Paktika Province, Afghanistan fixing generators, which I found to be a rewarding job overseas. Surrounded by all infantrymen, I listened to their stories of blood, guts, and gore. Their remembrances imparted to me left a strange empty hole inside. As I lay in a room that greatly resembled a dark, dreary cave, unable to sleep and thinking on my own tragedies, I sat up and began to write.

Notes

The Fatuous Kind

Fatuous people irritate me to no end;
Seems as though there's no way to make amend.
Being irrational is like having a dagger thrust into a lung;
Innocent bystanders just sit there and hold their tongue.
Frustration is sharp and quick, lingering a long while;
Visions of hostility then come about like pouring from a vile.
Inflicting pain for a smile on my face, a conundrum.
Let's just abandon this thought, tedium.
Wow, where did all this hostility come from?
Who have I now become?

Seclusion in the desert will rot a soul,
Turning the pleasant into a dark and dreary hole.
Once so much beauty was beheld here,
But now that time has passed—an infinite tear.
Moving on with one's self when change is unwanted,
Such a tough situation but optimism must be flaunted.
I can live with myself and learn to manage a short fuse.
I can learn to ignore the intellectually challenged so muse-
Realizing time is now of the essence;
No scowling, just learning to find the effervescence.

With an ecstatic demeanor (due to my being on R&R or a short vacation from deployment to Afghanistan,) I boarded an aircraft in Georgia bound for New York. A stewardess soon after approached me with concern from one of the other passengers. The fact that I was using my lighter to burn the loose threads on my uniform had an older couple upset. I rationalized with the stewardess; she smiled and then walked away.

Just when I thought that situation had been resolved and I could go back to planning the first day with my sons, the older couple began to get my attention. The lady said, "Sorry, ma'am, I mean that was so scary. Couldn't the lighter make us blow up, I mean!"

I quickly turned my head in amazement, and my blood began to boil. I wanted to ask the lady a few questions to evoke rational and logical thoughts. Maybe I could ask if she thought I was soaked in gasoline or had some other accelerant up my sleeve but instead, as the professional soldier I was trained to be, I kept my comments to myself and just began to write.

Notes

Afghanistan Beauty or Boils

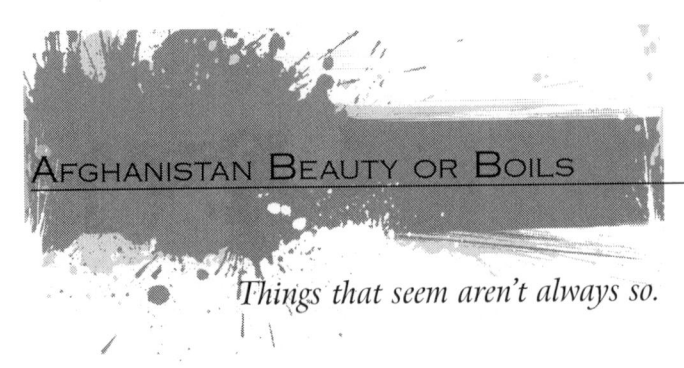

Things that seem aren't always so.

On my way to a land that seems nothing more than sand.
At a closer look, just take a glance,
One can see out here, there's a different kind of life and dance.
Not one that's dreadful or sad to push forth a tear,
Rather a wondrous marvel captured in a whirlwind of fear.

Life as it was so long ago,
Recent ages can ne'er behold,
The beauty of a way so simple and light,
Now to us seems shameful, with a dark and gruesome fight.
Those enemies who try to corrupt with an atrocious terror—
We, the US military soldiers, become the shearer.
Teaching Afghans right,
Training each and every day—
Making a way for these Afghans to once take back,
Their country and culture, no more to be jacked.
Nemeses disbanded- Freedom rings in a different way,
Making certain to destroy any and all Taliban protégé.

    I wrote this poem in my bed in Afghanistan. I was at the end of my tour and was reflecting on my experiences. I learned that we were making great strides in helping the Afghans regain order and control of their own country. Until you're there, fighting that war, you never really understand what it's about and what has been accomplished there.

I became astounded with the people, what they went through daily, both good and bad. I first thought the Afghan way of life, compared to modern civilization, seemed mundane and primitive. Yet, having lived there for a year with daily contact with them, I found a sweet innocence and a refreshing nature about the Afghans and how they viewed some things. Deploying to this strange yet astonishing country has opened my eyes by expanding my mind to a deeper, more meaningful, diverse and thankful outlook on life.

Notes

Treachery from Within

Today tells of tomorrow,
Though who really knows
Exactly what our future beholds?
Fortune, glory, things untold,
A mind-set then, taken back.
Commodities are what we lack.
Choppers heard flying overhead—
Riding in this combat truck, will some wind up dead?
So many meanings that can hold,
Trying to gain earnestly a courageous bold.
Looking out the window, stuck in a daze,
Wondrous mountains and cliffs crafting a maze—
Forty armored vehicles trudging through this terrain,
Trying to creep cautiously without pain.
Bloody and beaten or with mental damage concealed.
One or the other, maybe both are made real;
Fighting in a war is quite a big deal.
Though driving through this combat zone,
We're trained; professionals shouldn't groan.
Stiffen up and keep a keen eye;
That's how American Soldiers stay alive.

This poem is very special to me. It depicts the occurrence of traveling outside our F.O.B. walls and venturing into the rugged terrain of Afghanistan on a convoy.* I promised my family that while deployed, I wouldn't volunteer myself for any job that involved leaving the base. So when my platoon was asked for volunteers' to go on a convoy, I notably told my sergeant the promise I made to my family with a dejected gaze. He obviously understood my demeanor and tasked me out for the job. I happily accepted and was able to tell my family I didn't volunteer because technically, I didn't.

*Convoy: Many armored vehicles transporting troops, driving in a straight line from one base to another.

Notes

Life's Fear or Fate's Glory Tear

Here I am, flying so high;
Thoughts cross, by and by.
I can't, no, I'm not enough!
Damn, just stop the worries, be tough.
I've slept with a rifle bedside,
Lived by a code, though a lie.
I've seen death, natural and scandalous;
I've been a part of a crowd that vandalizes.
In short I've seen, laughed, and cried;
I've done everything but curiously confide.
So why not change this pace,
Grab for an exciting new race.
By doing that which I've always dreamed,
I'll set the example—there's more than to just be.

Your choice is how to control the tone;
Will you explore, create, or just groan?
Life thrives on what we make it.
Fears, tears, or a hollow pit—
Time to make an ultimate choice:
Will you keep silent or be a voice?
Aspirations need to be explored;
On your deathbed, you may be floored.
At world's end, your mind, body, and soul
No longer will be left an empty and frail hole.
As your spirit soars high in the sky,
You'll look back and astoundingly wave good-bye,

All the while saying to yourself,
"I'm glad I didn't leave those things on a shelf."
Then being seen at the pearly white gates,
It will be said, "Well done, child, for you fulfilled your fate."

Notes

Cavernous Vile Remnants

What do you do when it's taken away?
Cry all alone, hidden beneath the day?
Watch each moment pass, distorted through a glass?
Rather take part in its end, facing a foul taste,
While shreds of decency linger somewhere still?
Freedom pokes through by thoughts of ending "it" with a pill.
"Touché." Seems mundane and a cheap, thoughtless thrill.
Now raging, an adrenaline rush–numbing bliss.
Stop, think, and find a resource to break the decayed hiss,
Forced to morph "it" into a learned, peaceful twist.

This poem tells of an incident I refer to as "it," which happened overseas in Afghanistan. It was life changing and frightening at best. As time went on, the memory didn't just fade away into an unrealistic image, as I'd hoped it would. I contemplated either seeking help or relying on my own strength to overcome the situation. I decided I needed to seek counseling (which lasted a short while), but some damage was irreversible. I had changed and corrupted certain relationships by merely keeping "it" all in, while inadvertently distancing myself from society, from life, from everyone and everything I thought I knew. Of course, my real saving grace came later—from above.

Notes

Anticipation Changing

Calm and set is this demeanor,
Making much keener.
Stars above kept a tale
Known as a warrior fighting without fail.
All done not for self, without glory or pride,
Brothers in arms right at their side.
Releasing the oppressed
Is a task with no rest.
Those on the outside, this is what they see—
Truth painted and told, anything but glee.
Soon homeward to be found;
All that was past now bound
Within one's heart and soul.
What's been done still takes a toll;
Reintegrating back to a life civilized,
Learning again those who hold ties,
To a soldier's life and career—
Making now, each moment happy a tear,
This may be done one day at a time.
Wiping away all the memories' grime,
Family and friends feel the anticipation.
Awaiting an exciting yet relaxing vacation.
No more to live each day in war with rifles,
To watch out for people who trifle.
Back in the States, fear is at ease,

But to all soldiers a requirement of thee:
Wherever your heart and key,
On your game you still must be.

One memorable day in Afghanistan, I hitched a helicopter ride with my captain and a few lieutenants. We flew in a Black Hawk. I looked out the window at the land beneath me, admiring the scenery. Some people might assume I'd be wondering, *Is this my last ride? Will I die?* But on the contrary, my thoughts were about the experience in general, having been like so many other soldiers, numb to the dangers of the land. My mind then raced with thoughts. I wondered, *is it possible to put these crazy memories of war behind me? Will I just go on with life like nothing has ever happened, as if this past year has meant nothing? Will I see my family and loved ones differently? Will they notice differences in my personality?*

Just then, my thoughts trailed to a happy and exciting place, which was plastered on my face. Soon we'd all be home, some with amazing stories to tell. I wondered how it would feel. A thought then reentered my mind: dangers are not dismissed once we're back on American soil; they just change and rearrange.

As the chopper touched down, my thoughts trailed to our surroundings—we were blinded by the dust cloud and touched down at an angle before we leveled out and completely landed. With my twisted sense of humor, I found it hilarious but the whole experience really bothered my captain. As she eagerly departed the Black Hawk she exclaimed,

"You're not right Nero,"

Notes

INNER PEACE NOW UNLEASHED

Courage and strength; a fight within one's soul

Lying under a bench, I cringe
With the feeling of becoming unhinged,
So many instances of fear
Refusing to bring forth a tear.
I must settle in certain thoughts;
That which is done becomes a loss.
My mind's notion dissipates to let go;
The light has called a new show.
Recapture that which was wrought,
Days past I then fought
To keep my insides clean,
To keep my mind keen,
Staying sharp with a strong will.
Keeping the old seems to kill.
Knowing to start this path anew,
Rearranging my life in many ways too.
I won't let what's been done get me down,
No more aimless to wonder and frown.
Resetting my program, now needing thirst,
This must happen or I could burst.
So here I lay to think and repent,
Nothing to hold onto but a dent—
That's now my view of the past.
Time for moving on, finally, at last.
My spirit no longer hidden beneath a mask.

So much to do, such a big task;
Help I require for this journey.
Feels almost like lying on a gurney.
My place is optimism and drive;
Only then will I be truly alive.
By in so doing, hope and peace I will soon find
Within my soul, body, and mind.

Living for one year in close quarters with the same people can wear on a person. You work together seven days a week. You see them at the showers, at the chow hall, and in your living quarters. A soap opera forms, and that which was once real and true no longer matter. Finding a safe haven is the way to survive—just smile, keep to yourself and drive on. Work is the only thing that matters. Do your job and do it well. That's a soldier's drive when his or her world feels empty; soldier up and drive on. Distance will make a peaceful rest.

Notes

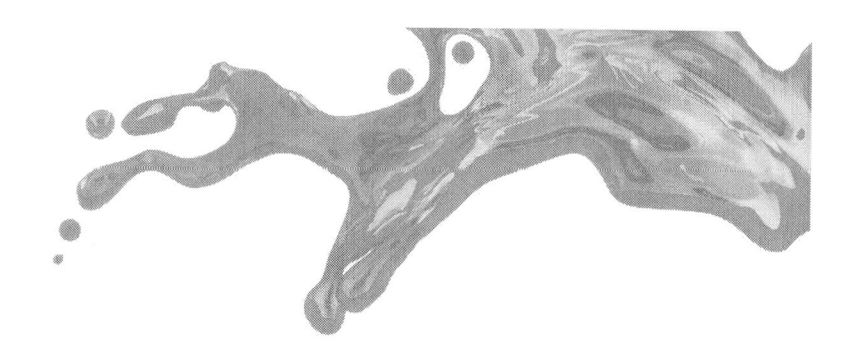

Basic Combat Training

Our Own Fight

Today I started a new life.
I knew it wouldn't be nice.
The tunnel looks long, dark, and dreary.
Though commonly known, the end's lit up—
Warm and bright, mostly without strife.
This journey's like cutting into bone with a knife.
Hard and tedious; seems like a roll of the dice.
Looking left and right, one gets so leery,
But hey, it's just like having a wife:
She's a lot of work, time, and money spent.
Look into your head ... ouch, what a dent!
Dig deep inside; find your reasons for it.
Never give up; just learn to bite the bullet.
Life's many choices, know you're in control.
The battlefield's in your mind, so fight, fight, fight.
This can be a helpful tip:
All hours of the night and during sunlight,
Fight, fight, fight—never give up!
With all your might, just fight!
Thinking on the reasons that you're here,
Reflecting back, the cause for what you did.
That's your fuel, so just stay positive,
Learning to release your fear,
For then all will become clear.
Your best will shine forth,
So be content with no remorse.

I wrote this poem in the beginning of Basic Combat Training (BCT). Many females were having trouble. Typically the issues were missing their families, dealing with all the physical training, and being told they were worthless garbage all day long. I wasn't having as rough a time as most of them though. I had a friend who was a drill sergeant, plus many family members who served in the military. Needless to say, my perspective on the whole situation was quite a bit calmer and more stable than most of the others. I wanted to lift their spirits, so I began to write and formed this poem in the dead of night using a flashlight to see what I was writing, hidden beneath the blankets on my bunk.

Notes

Madness

Today I saw this woman,
Though more fitting, liar!
She's evil through and through;
Reminds me of a dark and hot fire.
Not yellow or blue but black—what is she doing?
I bet her heart is shattered and oppressed, spreading deceitfulness and ruin.
Doesn't she know this life, it's serious?

No games can help when there are needs to be met.
No games create a life well spent.
No games can fix the brokenhearted.
No games should be played with a person to scar them.
This liar will pay! How, no one can tell;
This liar will live a life of hell.
What's given is always dished out in return.
God help her; such a hard lesson to learn.
It's not of my doing, nor of yours;
Fate will close her doors forevermore.

One female in BCT really made me red-hot mad. She started a rumor that one of our drill sergeants acted inappropriately with her. She was an obnoxious, thick, selfish person. Anyone who's been through BCT knows these traits will bring attention to you. It's like wearing a sign for all the drill sergeants to see that states, "Mess with me, please. I'm an easy target!"

Of course this soldier recruit was the center of many jokes and smoking sessions (physical exercise for punishment). She got tired of it, and instead of fixing herself, she formed a plot against the drill sergeant.

I know all this firsthand because I was on the other side of the locker when she was talking about it to other soldier recruits. Needless to say, justice was served—and I got a great poem out of the whole thing.

Notes

FASHIONED JUST RIGHT

In a bikini, watching lifeguard Ben,
Heels are together, feet flat on the floor again!
Kickin' back at the beach, with a drink in hand,
Just can't forget, no matter the land.
All those BCT things, ground in so tight,
Like a horse's bit, fitting in just right.
So long ago, it's as if a dream,
Evident by changes and learning a team.
Back so many years in the regular army,
Basic Combat Training holds the key:
Programmed and fashioned just right,
Forever and always, an American Soldier to be.

I wrote this poem while perched atop my bunk in basic training. I was reflecting on how the last few weeks changed me and about what our Drill Sergeants had stated earlier that day- that becoming a soldier was inevitably forever altering one's behaviors. I began putting pen to paper and had fun with my thoughts about what I'd be doing in a few months. Little did I know that right after BCT I'd be overseas in Afghanistan and not on some dream vacation.

Notes

Hasty Decisions

Throughout life there are choices to make;
It's as if stuck in a bottomless lake.
As we step into a new phase in life,
We become unsure and toil with strife.
This decision was made without thought;
Now the feeling becomes nothing more than caught.
Back and forth my mind wanders;
If I'd done the other, I'd be at peace and without ponders.
Now with my dreams and thoughts worn,
Guess I'll just sit and mourn.
Reflection brings the thought of things happening for a reason;
I'll have to wait this out for a season.
In my head I'm tormented with the thought to say,
This will all change one fine day.
I've learned my lesson quite well:
Don't be so quick to do, show, or tell.
Stop and consider; think before you decide.
Then next time I can effusively enjoy life's ride.

Realizing that a choice you made might have been a mistake can create such an abysmal feeling of failure. This I've realized firsthand, but it is not in reference to joining the military.

While in basic training, another MOS (Military Occupational Specialty) captivated my thoughts. I contemplated changing the trade I had signed up for but soon realized it was too late.

Learning to live with your choice can be difficult, but it is quite pertinent for happiness. The key is to look past what's been done and realize the future can still hold many incredible marvels. Nevertheless, I am glad that I stuck with being a generator mechanic and I wouldn't trade the experiences I've had, "for the world!"

Notes

Man Up

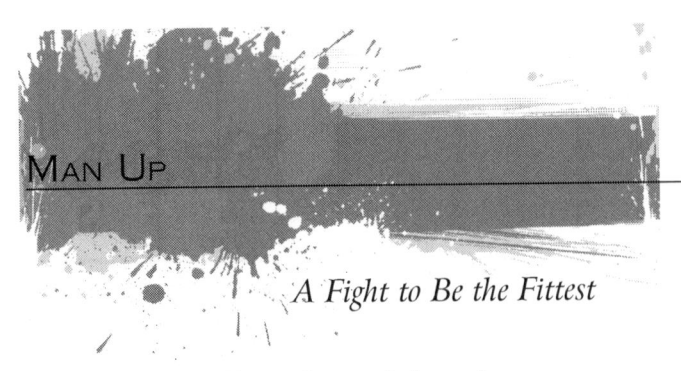

A Fight to Be the Fittest

This morning I awoke and found
My civilian ways, all were bound.
Looking through glass, this new man I see,
Straight-faced and no more just a she.
I never thought today would be;
American soldier is a new title for me.
How did it all happen—BCT!
My instructors are sergeants, drillin' us into the ground;
Through their snares and games, mental toughness is found.
Learning to shoot, fight, and kill;
Being a true warrior takes such a strong will.
Placing the mission first,
Stressing not to wind up in a hearse,
Never give up or accept defeat,
These our drill sergeants stomp to the beat.
They live their lives for this country free,
Teaching and mentoring, such a noble fee.
Selfless service, an important key.
Loyalty, duty, and respect,
Our drill sergeants give nothing short of their best.
Honor, integrity, and personal courage,
They, our example, have no rest.
Because of our drill sergeants and their persistent way,
We'll withstand the ultimate test one day.
Breaking us down just to build back up,

Surprise—we didn't split, rather true for most,
The one thought in training, so go ahead and boast:
You made it through; congrats and digest—
How shall we say, can't tell for the rest,
Did they even try to give their best?

Finding one's own personal best and surpassing that is the key to success in BCT which is specifically stated by the drill sergeants and trainers. Man's natural instinct though is to contort training into a competition which can spoil the atmosphere and/or destroy one's self-image. Those who were most successful learned to dismiss this distortion, adopt the teamwork concept and keep their sights fixed on the prize at the end of the tunnel- Graduation and earning the title of American Soldier.

Notes

Army Owned

Drill sergeants are a special breed,
Though at first sight it doesn't seem,
They do possess all one needs,
For soon, American Soldiers to be.
Some shaped from rotted clay,
Others come from demise in their hiding place.
Critiqued and fashioned the army way—
Strong willed and purpose driven,
That's how we start livin'.
Bold and brassy, fearing no more,
It's our nation that we fight for.
Our bodies no longer are our own,
Though this contract is just a loan.
Creating us warriors eventually to kill,
Our actions are by our own free will.

I wrote this poem after basic training in AIT (Advanced Individual Training). Here, soldiers learn to do the job that they chose. As I sat in my room, I thought about where we all came from and how we changed. We were no longer civilians. Selling our services as protectors and warriors comes at such a great price. Here, life starts as a new being, contracting your body out for a greater good. The thought of how this all came about and how incredible our drill sergeants were to take on that task then flooded my mind. "Army Owned" was inexorably born.

Notes

Born and Bred American Soldier

Now you've just walked in our door;
It's time to meet the Devil Dogs,
And the army's what we live for.
Don't think in here you'll get an easy ride—
Hell no! We'll make you sweat, bleed, or die.
It's more rewarding than an ice cold beer;
We'll weed out the weak ones and make you fear.
Now remember our company, known as the Mustangs;
Our bravery cuts deeper than a two-edged blade.
It was born from the warrior ethos,
Instilled by the army values,
Then drilled in by sergeants to boast,
Using physical training till you're cooked like a roast.
It's here the broke become shattered,
Forever to live tattered,
But the strong grow free;
American soldiers we shall be.

I wrote this poem in the middle of basic training at Fort Leonard Wood, Missouri. Lying on the top bunk with my legs dangled off the side, I was dazed in thought. *Devil Dogs, our platoon, Mustangs, our company—what are we about?* I thought to myself. Soon the words flew from my mind, "Born and Bred American Soldier" was formed.

The next day our platoon was getting smoked outside the DEFAC (dinning facility.) As we did push-ups until we collapsed, one of my battle buddies (another soldier recruit) talked me into handing this poem into our drill sergeant and that evening I followed through. Later I was informed that "Born and Bred American Soldier" was to be painted on our training bay wall! Sadly our company was disbanded and my poem was never showcased until now.

Notes

Freedom Killers

Fighting for freedom,
That's how we roll.
We are the military, takin' control.
Known as the baddest you've ever seen,
Lockin' and loadin' our magazine.
Shoot shoot shoot- shoot 'em full of lead.
Now look here; no stoppin' till they're dead.
Our nation, this we'll proudly defend,
Strong and true, to the horrid end.

Notes

Flying High

Graduation

*101st Airborne;
Screaming Eagles
Hooah!*

The Beauty of Afghanistan

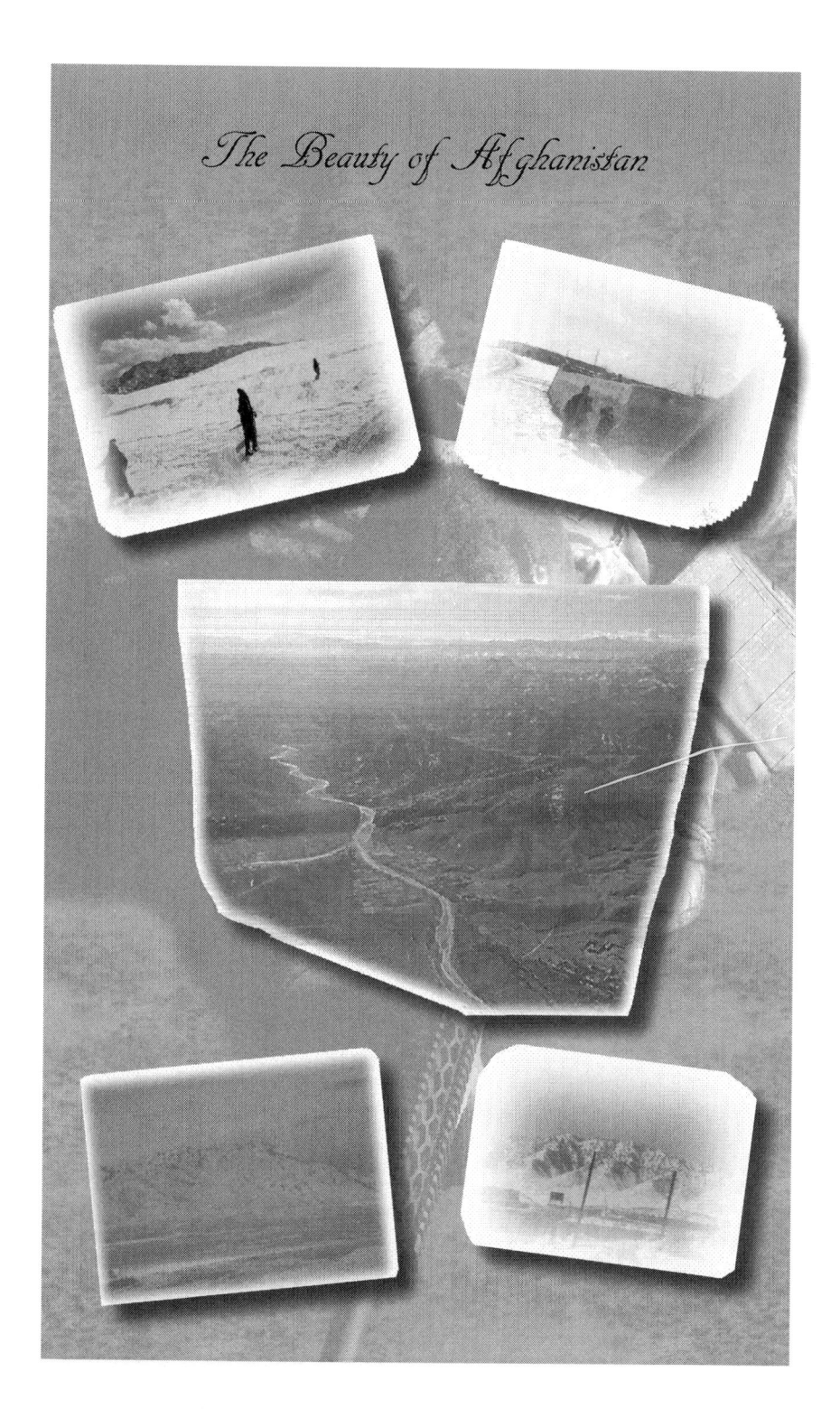

Cultures Collide

Playing while mommy's away

*On our way to the Christmas Market
Celebration in Germany*

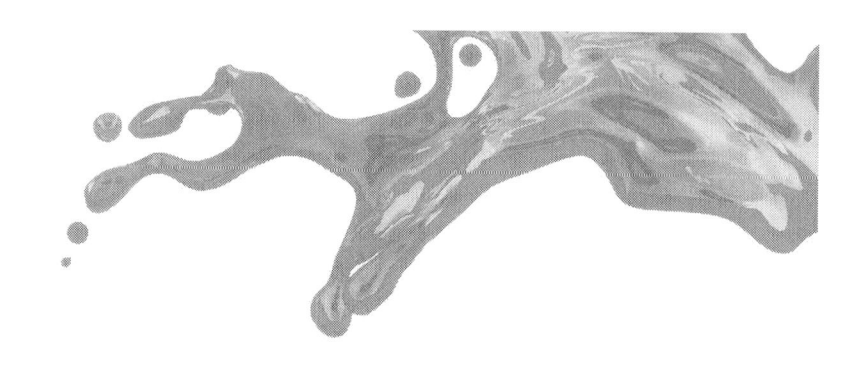

The Transcendent

Epiphany's Edge

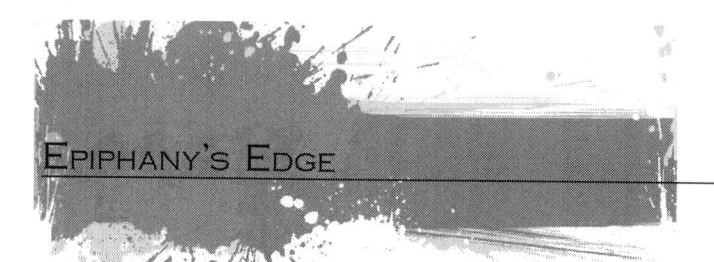

My heart delights in the thought of you,
Contemplating and fantasizing dreams anew.
For by revealing love springs forth a vision,
Joyously melodic to rejuvenate the incision.
Life—a song making happy or sad, causing a sever,
Seems to be living with duty-filled leverage.
Peer down to see the past and post so prominent—
Looking off this ledge, refreshed a quickening instant.
Clear direction comes now, needing a suture,
This epiphany has revealed its future.
Learning to divide the pure from its whore,
Releasing thoughts of enduring heartaches that matter no more.
'Tis all worthwhile for a glorious finish to meditate and say
Love was found to be the one and only true way.

Notes

A Joyful Tale

When the sun shines bright, high in the sky,
A thought of you then crosses my mind—
My family, my love, the apple of my eye.
A tear I then shed,
For I'd rather be with you instead.

My heart grows dark like a river in black,
With you so far, a heart's warmth I lack.
So I'll change my thoughts to days gone past;
A joyful heart within my soul then beats, alas.

The memories of you I eagerly behold;
A happiness can now peacefully unfold.
Laughing and playing while in my midst,
Joking and roughhousing, till the night calls it quits.

Once more soon a story's end,
A new beginning I must mend.
Moving here and staying there
Always creates a longing and tear.
So this now I see,
An exciting new chapter to be—
Infinitely destined to live out our happily ever after.

Soon I'm coming home to end this task;
No more hiding behind a mask.

Work becomes raising my family, this I confide:
Bursting with pride to be finally, forever at your side.

As I sat and reminisced about the last year and a half of my life devoted to the military, I realized I spent most of it separated from my sons. I joined the US Army and went to basic training. From there I spent a few more months in training, learning my job as a generator mechanic in AIT. Soon after, I was stationed at Fort Campbell, Kentucky, but only to find out once I got there that we were deploying to Afghanistan right away.

I didn't mind going overseas to fight; it's what I signed up for. What bothered me was that once again I'd have to endure a long stretch of time away from my sons. All this considered, after I touched down in the foreign country depression quickly set in.

One night, after work, I sat on the edge of my bed, bewildered at my situation. Then I thought, *well ... roll with the punches,* and out came yet another poem. It didn't take the sting away, but it helped to dull the pain of separation a bit.

Notes

A Memory's Whisper

Walking through the night's mist,
Longing for her true love's kiss.
Thinking on days past and gone,
Striving for future goals, never to pawn—
A love so pure befalling disruption and torment,
Now never to encounter her and his passion.
The whisper of a moment is where that memory lives,
Forever thankful for even a glance into that abyss.
Real or not, no one will ever know.
Adjust from that experience, an enlightening glow.
Now and always will her countenance show
That of a love she'll never know.

Notes

A Heart's Mend

Regrets cannot surpass that which has been done.

Throughout life are unexpected turns,
Proven continuous and may cause burns.
The needed ointment that can heal
Should first the outer edge peel.
Cleansing comes through many steps;
All the while, keep a heartfelt bounce and some Schweppes.*
Now around the bend-
A joyous thought and happy end.
Till more advances move your way,
Keep in mind that very same day,
Where you've been and what you've seen,
How you've healed, never again shows keen.
Something new and soul-wrenching tart
Can always be formed into a pure and sweet heart.

*Schweppes is a brand name of ginger ale.

I wrote this poem in Italy. I was on my way to Afghanistan with my unit 2/506 FSC from the 101st Airborne Division. We made a pit stop at the airport there. It was quite lame to be in a new country, all the while being confined to seeing miles of runways and dozens of planes but not authorized to venture out into the unknown country.

Italy is known as one of the most romantic countries in the world, yet loneliness mixed with pride began to overrun my brain as I sat and gazed out the window. Adorned in my uniform and combat boots, I found myself ripping apart my soul, reflecting on where I'd been, as opposed to where I was at that present time. My fingers began to fly as my head filled and regurgitated past and present feelings.

Notes

Memories End

Winter is sprung, quick as night falls as a tear;
Green fades and glistening white blankets appear.
A chill fills the air, though smiles are now broad;
The breath is seen as a cloud of fog.
Soon a cold laughter becomes the sound of night;
Hot cocoa and steaming soup comfort the soul's fight.
A quickening likeness of days past touches the warmth of skin;
Familiar faces now linger in the bottle of gin.
Those we miss still thrive deep within one's leer,
While memories surpass fears,
The day's end is near.

One early evening, I was sitting on the edge of my bed in Landstuhl, Germany. I felt lost; it was Christmas time, and I was thousands of miles away from my family, both in the States and in Afghanistan. I began to think of others who were alone at this holiday season and wondered how they could be comforted with no kin of any kind around them. I also had contemplated those who had lost loved ones permanently and thought, *At least I know I'll get to see mine again.* A strong echo then rang in my ears: *Write. I need to write.* As I put pen to paper, my soul felt lighter. Within minutes, "Memories End" was born and my spirit was instantly revived.

Notes

Love's Cruel Passion

Can love be found after betrayal?
No one knows the answer; so contemplate to induce prevail …

Love is tangible thoughts trod on by distractions,
Only to take a dagger and deceive, signified now with pain and your heart in fractions.

Earnestly believing again, cutting through its cast—
A familiar love known to your soul, once defined to surpass,
Distant memories now beguile quite fast.

Cascading down into a darkening, infinite hole,
Maybe it's stuck on a desert island, perched on a lonesome pole,
Same as trying to sift through hot ash and burned coal.

Do you drop it off at the next stop, never to look back?
Remember it as a worthless, rusted tack?
Foreseeing emotions weigh you down, a choking slack.

To and fro thoughts continually pour in.
Live or die? Depends on your good or evil twin—
Destiny made by decisions or play,
Think realistically and listen closely; don't be late.

Mindful of your intuition to clear the way,
Broken from the inside out, a high price to pay.
Nothing is certain except your date,
Worrisome of its crashing fate.

It's your life; do with it what you will.
Your emotions and body fervently kill;
Realizing this is not just a thrill,
Possibly to regret a quickened end,
All this now is beheld- a great passion continually to mend.

Kimberly Mae

Notes

Inept Dreams

So here I am again,
Words that won't come to an end.
The thoughts that clutter my brain
Make me rethink, am I sane?
A moment's flash, thinking I know
Just how to unify and stow
These retentions trapped in my bar.
I shudder to debate afar;
Reformation could change this fate.
Should I realize this moment's bait?
Potentially twisted, a broken link,
The reformed ripples' ink
Needs to be stopped and turned about.
Shanty abodes, tranquil thought,
All would be fine left to be naught,
If only I had tried and fought.
Realizing now I'll never know
The glories of what I might have owned.

Maladroit fantasies can reinforce a person's creativity and commonsensical thinking. As a child, so many of these inept dreams are shattered by negative influences biased by their own heartaches and fears. This poem imparts a regretful reality to those innocent dreamers expressing these devastations and to say, "Never give up on your dreams."

Notes

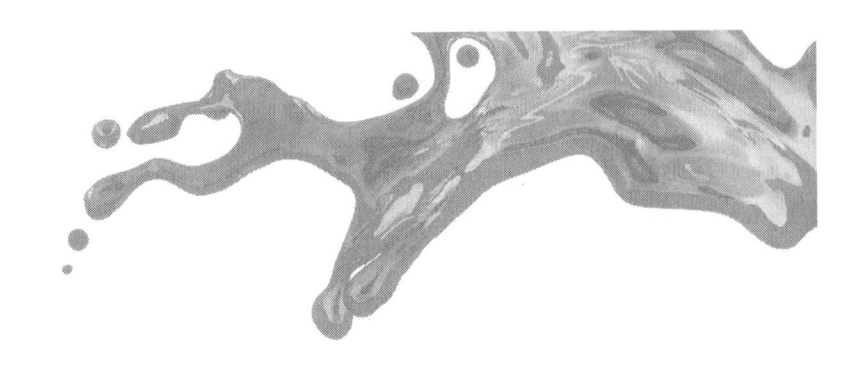

A Special Thanks

Incessant Love

Today, looking back,
You are what I lack.
So many fond memories,
Pure as an elephant's tusk, ivory.

Smiles I do so fondly recall;
You picked me up with each fall.
All you asked was a word of thanks;
So long since I filled that tank.

May I say how proud I am?
Not to be confused with a sham.
I sincerely do say and show
All these things you must know,
For within my heart there is no lie,
And you see through me, by and by.

A frail little girl once I was;
You strengthened me right then, just because.
True love surely has no bounds;
This you've shown to be profound.

Still in awe with each passing moment
That you so willingly did an atonement,
For so undeserving I may be,
You said it's no matter, for you paid the fee.

People say love, true as it may seem,
But you've shown me we're a team.
Remarkable and carefree,
Strong like a steadfast rooted tree.
Forever and always, this is my plea:
My homage and life I now give thee.

Kimberly Mae

Notes

Bittersweet

Living for Jesus,
Not just to please us.
Give your life wholly;
You could become a goalie,
Blocking sins from entering in.
Let this be something you teach your kin;
To be sure, use your body and head.
Think—is this biblical or just dead?
Carnal thinking is where it begins.
When that happens, drop to your shins;
Pray for cleansing and power.
Don't give in this hour.
Learn to start there
And be strong like a bear.
Eventually your carnality will fade;
It's that simple, been done and paid.
So thank Jesus—he did the hard part.
Our role is sweet, but his was disturbingly tart.

Notes

"People, even more than things, have to be restored, renewed, revived, reclaimed and redeemed. Never throw out anyone."
—Audrey Hepburn

"The Journey of a thousand miles begins with a single step."
—Lao Tzu

Made in the USA
Middletown, DE
31 October 2019